What other about this book

It's never too late to begin reading to, and with, your child. The 6th edition of 101 Reasons to READ with Your Child conveys both how and why in fast, easy dosages for busy parents and caregivers.
Emily Kirkpatrick, Vice President
National Center for Family Literacy

The love for reading starts at home and 101 Reasons to READ With Your Child highlights why. Every parent would benefit from reading it.
Shelley Morehead, Program Administrator
Pizza Hut BOOKIT! National Reading Incentive Program

If you have ever read to a child, you know what a treat that is for the adult. This book makes clear why that shared moment is life-giving for the child. A compelling argument for making reading together a habit.
Daniel Domenech, Executive Director, AASA
The School Superintendents Association

101 Reasons to READ With Your Child can help change the trajectory for young people who struggle to read throughout their schooling. These students often leave school without a diploma at huge costs to the individual and to the nation as a whole.
Bob Wise, President,
The Alliance for Excellent Education
Former Governor of West Virginia

I am absolutely convinced by your 101 Reasons to READ to Your Child. In fact, I'd add one more: It's fun.
Walter Anderson, Chairman and Publisher
Parade Publications

So many wonderful reasons to read with your child! For military parents deployed halfway around the world, the opportunity to read to their children is available and all 101 reasons still prevail! For these deployed military parents, reading a storybook will ease the stress of separation, will make reunions and homecomings easier, will allow for the deployed mom or dad to parent from afar, and will cultivate a love of reading – just like this book says! What a terrific compilation!
Sally Ann Zoll, Ed.D., CEO
United Through Reading

The research cited in 101 Reasons to Read confirms the importance of reading with children to ensure academic success, but the Reasons are where the rubber meets the road. Parents will easily find a Reason they relate to, and be compelled to grab a book or e-reader, sit down with their little reader and share the gift of reading.
Mary M. Keller, Ed.D., President and CEO
Military Child Education Coalition

101 Reasons To Read With Your Child provides parents and care-givers with the compelling impact that reading to children will have on their development, and hard facts that point to the outcomes that result from an illiterate society. Read this guide and read to your children – every day.
Marcie Craig Post, Executive Director
International Reading Association

Research has shown that family involvement in their children's education is the single factor that correlates most strongly with success in school. Parent involvement can take many forms, but none is more important than reading with a child, and this book provides 101 compelling reasons why that is so.
Bill Milliken, Author of The Last Dropout and From the Rearview Mirror, and **Founder of Communities In Schools**

A child's journey to become a reader starts early. 101 Reasons to Read to Your Child reminds us that cultivating a love of reading in children can ultimately provide the foundation for their future success. This is a wonderful resource for anyone who has a child in their life.
Jess Lazzara, Vice President of Program
Jumpstart

101 Reasons to Read With Your Child" is an excellent resource for parents, and even teachers and educators. It offers easy-to-do tips in a clear and effective way, and aligns with everything we try to accomplish at Books for Kids: to immerse children in a print-rich environment, and to read with children during their most formative years. These critical practices have been proven to lead to success in school, and in life.
Amanda Hirsh, Executive Director
The Books for Kids Foundation

All children need caring adults in their lives who read with them. This book makes a clear case for how enjoyable, rewarding, and important it is for all of us to fulfill this responsibility.
Ron Fairchild, President & CEO
Smarter Learning Group

In reading and re-reading your book, I take my hat off to you for the VERY thorough job you did and the various aspects on which you touched. Your book is MUCH, MUCH more than just 101 reasons to do a very common sense thing. I meant it when I said that your book should be required reading for reading teachers and parents. Your references are a key to anyone's desire to dig deeper.
Richard Sutz, CEO
The Literacy Company & the Institute For Efficient Reading

This book reminds parents of the many benefits that sharing books with children can bring. It will encourage parents who may have many books in their homes, as well as those who have few, to find creative ways to engage young children in vital, daily reading experiences that will transform their lives.
Darlene Kostrub, Chief Executive Officer
Palm Beach County Literacy Coalition

I firmly believe that reading is the theater of the mind and TV will never replace it. I have eleven great-grandchildren to get your book and follow its advice.
Art Linkletter, (Deceased)

This book is a great reminder of how important it is to read to our children. Not only does reading build close relationships, it opens new worlds to our children and encourages them to dream. What a great gift to give a child.
Dave Thomas, (Deceased) Founder
Wendy's Old Fashioned Hamburgers

101 Reasons to READ With Your Child can help teachers connect to parents in creative and delightful ways. Imagine how far we could go with reading if we used this book as the catalyst for conversation, both in and out of schools. I can't wait to put it to good use within our growing network of Oklahoma A+ Schools.
Jean Hendrickson, Executive Director
Oklahoma A+ Schools/University of Central Oklahoma

101 Reasons to READ With Your Child

Other Books
by StarGroup International

CITIZENSHIP: What Every American Needs to Know
(First Edition 2012)
(Second Edition 2013)

Hey Kids, America Needs Us!
(First Edition 2012)

101 Reasons to READ With Your Child
(First Edition 2000)
(Second Edition 2002)
(Third Edition 2009)
(Fourth Edition 2011)
(Fifth Edition 2012)
(Sixth Edition 2014)

101 Reasons to Be a Proud American
(2001)

Celebrating AMERICA
(2004)

History of The The DEMOCRATIC Party
(2004)

History of The The REPUBLICAN Party
(2004)

101 Reasons to READ With Your Child

Compiled by

Brenda Star

Sixth Edition

STAR
GROUP

BOOKS

StarGroup International, Inc. Book Division
West Palm Beach, Florida

Sixth Edition 2014

Coordinated by Brenda Star
Contrubutors: Shawn McAllister, Cheryl Kravetz, Jane Evers, J.F. Butler,
  Gary Edelson and James A. Carter III
Senior Editor: Annaleah Morrow, Ph.D.
Cover and book design by Mel Abfier

Produced by Star Group International, Inc.
www.stargroupinternational.com

Printed in the United States of America

Library of Congress Card Number: Pending

101 Reasons to READ with Your Child
ISBN 978-1-884886-73-7

This book is available for quantity purchases, sales promotions, customization, premiums, fund-raising and educational use. For more information contact:

StarGroup International
1194 Old Dixie Highway, Suite 201
West Palm Beach, FL 33403
(561) 547-0667
www.stargroupinternational.com

Table of Contents

Readers Oath

I promise to read
Each day and each night,
I know it's the key
To growing up right.

I'll read to myself,
I'll read to a crowd.
It makes no difference
If silent or loud.

I'll read at my desk,
At home and at school.
On my bean bag or bed,
By the fire or pool.

Each book that I read
Puts smarts in my head,
Cause brains grow more thoughts
The more they are fed.

So I take this oath
To make reading my way
Of feeding my brain
What it needs every day.

Words by Debra Angstead, Missouri-National Education Association

Preface

Every night, parents are putting their children to bed by opening up their favorite picture books and reading aloud. They may not realize it, but they're paving the foundation for their child's academic achievement.

Through my work as President of Reading Is Fundamental, I've met countless children who've been so lucky. It's abundantly clear upon meeting them — with their rich vocabularies and their sharp young minds — that they're primed for success. Sadly, I've met countless others who will be spending years playing a game of catch-up. And no matter how hard a teacher works, bridging the gap that exists between them and their peers is only possible in most cases through two things: access to books and an engaged parent.

If you're not yet reading with your child, have no fear. In the following pages, you'll find tips, facts and statistics that can help you on your journey — a journey that's never too late to begin. Not only will your child's knowledge of printed letters and words grow, but your knowledge of each other will too. Whether you end up rhyming with *Fox in Socks* or spelling with *Charlotte's Web*, you'll be exploring new worlds together — sharing new adventures and experiences with every page you turn. And with each new story, you'll ultimately be writing a new chapter for your child's life — one richer in opportunities for success in school and life.

Carol Rasco
Executive Director, **Reading is Fundamental** (RIF)

Foreword

"Children are made readers on the laps of their parents."
--Emilie Buchwald

Most of us, when asked to name our first teacher, respond with the person who taught our kindergarten or first grade class.

But, of course, our first teacher knew us long before we entered school.

Even if we didn't realize it at the time, our first and most important teacher was the same person that taught us to hold a fork and to tie our shoes. Whoever that person was, be it parents or guardians, they spoke the words that we heard as a child and set the foundation for the person we have become today.

Learning begins at birth and blossoms in the home. It starts with highly-engaged parents who take the time to read to their children every single day.

The evidence is clear: children who are introduced to basic literacy skills in their infancy are more likely to start school on track (and stay on track) than those who arrive in kindergarten without exposure to books, language, or reading. On top of that, those children who are not fortunate enough to arrive prepared to read on the first day of kindergarten tend to fall behind as the school year progresses.

Proficiency in reading by the end of the third grade is a crucial marker in a child's education development. A stunning 68% of fourth graders enrolled in public schools were reading below proficiency levels in 2011, according to the Annie E. Casey Foundation's Kids Data Book.

At Reach Out and Read, we're working to change that percentage by distributing books to children and advice to parents about the importance of reading aloud. In pediatrician's waiting rooms, parents can find resources and sample children's books.

We are in the midst of an early education revolution. We're coming together as organizations, as communities, and as a nation to ensure that all children start school ready to read, learn, and succeed. I'm proud to stand beside others such as Brenda Star, the author of this book, to make sure we are doing everything we can for our children. This delightful book, 101 Reasons to READ With Your Child brings that important message to life.

So grab a storybook, and bring your little one to your lap. When you open a book together, you are opening the door to a bright future for your child.

Anne-Marie Fitzgerald
Executive Director of **Reach Out and Read**

For more tips on reading to young children,
please visit www.reachoutandread.org.

Introduction

Reading seems to fall into two main categories — that of survival or transportation. I see examples of these with my children. My 6-year-old is in that first survival reading category; he just wants to be able to read the prompts on the video screen to understand which Jedi Knights have the special powers he wants to use to win the game. My 9-year-old, on the other hand, is in the transportation reading category. He engrosses himself in the C.S. Lewis mystical world of Narnia, or fights the battles with Greek gods as he is transported to new places as he reads books about Greek mythology. My goal as a parent is to help foster a love of reading for my younger son so that he moves into the deeper transportation stage of reading.

I see these stages of reading with my college students as well. As a Business Communications professor, I ask my students to describe their passions within their class introductions. My informal research suggests that those who have listed reading as one of their passions are normally more successful in my class; they are more engaged with the material, and have an easier time applying the concepts we discuss and translating them to their real-world communication scenarios.

So, to borrow from the RIF program, reading is fundamental, but it is a gateway to so much more. This book offers only 101 reasons of probably thousands of benefits that can be gained for both you and your children when you participate in reading with them. We can take responsibility for our children's futures by being positive role models to them. Modern life runs in high gear, yet a family unit can redefine itself in today's terms and not lose the emotional foundations that keep it healthy.

How can this be done?

By reading with our children.

A half-hour of reading daily can reshape and improve the quality of family life for both parent and child. It can be the haven of peace in a hectic day. Reading can unite family members of all ages. I hope some of these reasons motivate you to find new ways to read with your child — perhaps you will even read more yourself.

Annaleah Morrow, Ph.d.

Education Administration,
College Professor, and Mother of two,
Senior Editor

Impact of eBooks

The research varies on the positive and negative aspects of electronic books (eBooks) for children; however, one thing is clear — eBooks are changing the way we read. eBooks can allow us to choose alternate endings in a book, provide interactive media such as pictures or, provide pop-up dictionary definitions, and even assist with word pronunciation.

Imagine a young reader interacting with an eBook filled with new words focused on phonetics. The eBook can not only provide moving pictures to engage and entertain the reader, but can help the child pronounce difficult words to master the new concepts. Amelia Moody found that "high quality interactive e-storybooks may support emergent literacy development . . . supporting vocabulary development, engagement, and comprehension of the story." Interactive storybooks also give young readers access to literature they might not be able to read independently because of their reading skills. On the other hand, eBooks of lower quality might inhibit learning, as they could offer "distracting digital features including animations and sounds unrelated to the story" (Moody).

A report funded by the US Department of Education, at Brown University, found that eBooks with the ability to provide feedback to readers was also helpful. They cited a 1997 study from Lewin, stating, "children using electronic talking books were able to read more independently possibly because the computer provided them with cues to cross-check meanings, and the colorful illustrations and animations motivated the children to use the program on their own. The children were also able to develop effective decoding strategies using the various components of the software, allowing them to read more of the text on their own."

The positive effects of eBooks may not be limited to young readers. A sixth-grade teacher (Grams) studied the effect of providing eBooks to his students, and was astounded at the increased number of books his students were reading. He noted that his students read more often without prompting, and shared how much they enjoyed being able to read in a dark room, or have the book available wherever the student happened to be.

Researchers are still determining if the effects of eBook-reading are as positive as when reading traditional printed material, but it is still important to understand this medium. While its positive effect on improving general literacy and entertainment reading seem to support eBooks, the negative reports seem to focus more on eBooks for academic studies. A study with an academic library and Sony found "complaints about [students'] inability to make in-text notes and easily navigate pages might point to the need to be close to their computers, notebooks, and other course materials while doing assigned readings on the devices." Our children have access to more literature today in the palm of their hand than is available in a single physical library.

References for eBook research

Behler, Anne. E-readers in action.
http://americanlibrariesmagazine.org/features/09242009/e-readers-action

Grams, David. E-Books: Motivating students to read independently,
http://www.goknow.com/GettingStarted/Documents/Grams_D_e-books.pdf

Moody, Amelia. PhD. Journal of Literacy and Technology,
http://www.literacyandtechnology.org/volume_11_4/JLT_V11_4_2_Moody.pdf

NEIR TEC Research, Funded by US Dept of Education,
http://www.neirtec.org/reading_report/report.htm

Schcolnik, Miriam. PhD Dissertation,
http://www.planetebook.com/downloads/schcolnik.pdf

Facts & Statistics

By the age of 2, children who are read to regularly display greater language comprehension, larger vocabularies, and higher cognitive skills than their peers

Each dropout, over his or her lifetime, costs the nation approximately $260,000.

http://www.bookspring.org/literacy-statistics/

We only have 2 percent of a child's lifetime to give them reading skills that will have an impact on them for the remaining 98% of their lives.

http://www.edu-cyberpg.com/Literacy/stats.asp

The U.S. is the only country among 20 OECD (*Organization for Economic Co-operation and Development*) free-market countries where the current generation is not as well educated than the previous one.

34 million adults function at below basic literacy levels, meaning they are unable to complete simple literacy tasks such as filling out a job application, fill out a deposit slip or read a prescription label.

http://www.famlit.org/media-resources/statistics/

Two thirds of students, who cannot read proficiently by the end of the 4th grade, will end up in jail or on welfare.
85% of all juveniles who interface with the juvenile court system are functionally illiterate.

Illiteracy and crime are closely related. The Department of Justice states, "The link between academic failure and delinquency, violence, and crime is related to reading failure." Over 70% of inmates in America's prisons cannot read above a fourth grade level.

Many of the USA ills are directly related to illiteracy. Literacy is learned. Illiteracy is passed along by parents who cannot read or write. One child in four grows up not knowing how to read. Low literacy costs $73 million per year in terms of direct health care costs. A recent study by Pfizer put the cost much higher.

http://www.begintoread.com/research/literacystatistics.html

Research suggests that quality parent-child interaction is important for children's development of literacy.

Families and parents in particular, play an important role in this process. For decades, research has shown the children whose parents read to them become better readers and perform better in school.

Reading aloud to young children is not only one of the best activities to stimulate language and cognitive skills; it also builds motivation, curiosity, and memory.

Early language skills, the foundation for reading ability and school readiness, are based primarily on language exposure - resulting from parents and other adults talking to young children.

The nurturing and one-on-one attention from parents during reading aloud encourages children to form a positive association with books and reading later in life.

Reading aloud is a proven technique to help children cope during times of stress or tragedy.

Reading difficulty contributes to school failure, which increases the risk of absenteeism, leaving school, juvenile delinquency, substance abuse, and teenage pregnancy - all of which perpetuate the cycles of poverty and dependency.

Children who were read to frequently are nearly twice as likely as other children to show three or more skills associated with emergent literacy.

Reading aloud stimulates language development even before a child can talk.

Activities such as reading are usually "very child-centered, are conducted in a relaxed atmosphere, and allow for a warm, positive interaction between children and their parents.

A typical child from a low-income family enters kindergarten with a listening vocabulary of 3,000 words, while a typical child of a higher income family enters with a listening vocabulary of 20,000 words.

http://www.reachoutandread.org/impact/importance.aspx

Reading motivation activities, books in the home, leisure reading, and parent involvement are among the best ways to help children develop into capable readers and decrease the risk of educational failure.

http://www.rifpittsburgh.org/Facts-Statistics

More than 75% of those on welfare, 85% of unwed mothers and 68% of those arrested are illiterate. 60 % of America's prison inmates are illiterate and 85% of all juvenile offenders have reading problems.

Many adults in the U.S. can't read well enough to read a simple story to a child.

Children who have not developed some basic literacy skills by the time they enter school are 3 to 4 times more likely to drop out in later years.

To participate fully in society and the workplace in 2020, citizens will need powerful literacy abilities that until now have been achieved by only a small percentage of the population.

50 percent of American adults are unable to read an eighth grade level book.

It is estimated that the cost of illiteracy to business and the taxpayer is $20 billion per year.

56 percent of young people say they read more than 10 books a year, with middle school students reading the most. Some 70 percent of middle school students read more than 10 books a year, compared with only 49 percent of high school students.

Out-of-school reading habits of students have shown that even 15 minutes a day of independent reading can expose students to more than a million words of text in a year.

http://www.readfaster.com/education_stats.asp#literacystatistics

The US Census Bureau reports that "adults 18 and over with a master's, professional or doctoral degree earned an average of $79,946, while those with less than a high school diploma earned about $19,915." Adults with a "bachelor's degree earned an average of $54,689 in 2005 while those with a high school diploma earned $29,448.

To determine how many prison beds will be needed in future years, some states actually base part of their projection on how well current elementary students are performing on reading tests.

"One in every 100 U.S. adults 16 and older is in prison or jail in America (about 2.3 million in 2006). About 43 percent do not have a high school diploma or equivalent, and 56 percent have very low literacy skills.

http://literacyprojectfoundation.org/community/statistics/

A mother's [lack of] reading skills is the greatest determinant of a child's future academic success, outweighing other factors, such as neighborhood and family income.

http://www.odl.state.ok.us/literacy/statistics/family.htm

Children spend five times as much time outside the classroom as they do in school, so parents and caregivers must be equipped to support their learning.

http://www.national-coalition-literacy.org/advocacy/Family
LiteracyFactSheetfromNCFL.pdf

A single year of parental education has a greater positive impact on the likelihood of a son or daughter attending a postsecondary institution than does an extra $50,000 income.

http://www.national-coalition-literacy.org/advocacy/
FamilyLiteracyFactSheetfromNCFL.pdf

What is Reading?

Reading is a complex system of deriving meaning from print that requires all of the following:

- The skills and knowledge to understand how phonemes, or speech sounds, are connected to print.

- The ability to decode unfamiliar words.

- The ability to read fluently.

- Sufficient background information and vocabulary to foster reading comprehension.

- The development of appropriate active strategies to construct meaning from print.

- The development and maintenance of a motivation to read.

The five components of reading:

- Phonemic awareness: the ability to notice, think about, and work with the individual sounds in spoken words.

- Phonics: the relationships between the letters (graphemes) of written language and the individual sounds (phonemes) of spoken language. Phonics instruction teaches learners to use these relationships to use and write words.

- Fluency: the ability to read a text accurately and quickly. When fluent readers read silently, they recognize words automatically. They group words quickly to help them gain meaning from what they read. They read aloud effortlessly and with expression.

Fluency is important because it provides a bridge between word recognition and comprehension.

- Vocabulary: refers to the words we must know to communicate effectively. Vocabulary is also very important to reading comprehension. Readers cannot understand what they are reading without knowing what most of the words mean. Learning to read more advanced texts means readers must learn the meaning of new words that are not part of their oral vocabulary.

- Comprehension: the reason for reading. If readers can read the words but do not understand what they are reading, they are not really reading. Good readers are both purposeful (they have a reason to read) and active (they think to make sense of what they read).

http://www.nifl.gov/research/researchdef.html?print=true

Reading Tips

Tips for Reading with Children

- Give your children something to look forward to by reading to them every day, and at the same time if possible.

- Have your children read out loud to you.

- Listen carefully, and make sure to praise your children's reading.

- Even after your children can read on their own, keep reading to them so they can enjoy stories and books that interest them but are too hard for them to read by themselves.

- Visit the public library often. Most libraries sponsor summer reading clubs with easy goals for preschool, primary and elementary students.

- Ask questions: Who were the main characters? What happened? What part of the book did they like best? Remember not to drill children too much on novel content. Summer reading should foster reading for pleasure.

- Provide incentives and set an example by reading yourself.

- If you read aloud, read with expression to hold the child's interest.

- Don't read too fast.

- Choose books that you or your child are excited about – enjoy what you read.

- If you are reading a book for the first time, scan it to get a feel for it before reading it with your child.

- Make reading part of your everyday routine; encourage your child to read.

- Have books on hand at home.

- Encourage your child to cherish books by giving them a safe place of their very own.

- Stay in touch with your child's teacher and know what books they are reading in the classroom.

- Let your child read his/her favorite book or read subjects that interest him/her.

- Praise the child for her/his efforts in reading.

- Encourage your child to read many different kinds of stories, books, magazines and comics.

- Listen to audio books.

- Talk to your child about her/his favorite books, and ask what their friends are reading.

- Talk to your child about his/her favorite authors and stories.

- Use reading to get information; use sources such as the Yellow Pages, Internet, the dictionary, cookbooks & encyclopedia.

- Play word games such as Scrabble or Boggle.

- Let your child read with younger brothers or sisters.

- Have a discussion with your child about the meaning of what you are reading together.

For specific activities you can do with your child go to: http://ed.gov/parents/academic/ help/reader/part5.html

And now...
101 Reasons
to
READ
With Your Child

1

Encourages Bonding

Bonding is the ability to trust one another implicitly. Intimate contact while reading with your family can become the basis for this trust. Bonding on a daily basis makes the private time with our children a source of comfort. When they have doubts and questions, they will know we are there for them.

Bridges the Generation Gap

2

Reading together gives us the opportunity to extend ourselves and our love to our children. During difficult times it can draw us together. Shared reading time is a great time to discuss issues with our children. Whether or not we agree with them, reading helps us find a way to solve problems and deal with issues together, as a family.

3 Encourages Character Development

One way to teach character development is through exposure to good characters from great books.

Explains the Meaning of Success 4

Commitment, goals and hard work... these concepts become understandable to children of all ages when they read stories about the success of others.

5 Builds Self-Confidence

We feel good about ourselves and our family ties when we spend time reading together.

Teaches Responsibility

6

The concept of "taking responsibility" is one that needs to be strengthened by parental advice during our children's formative years. Reading helps prepare our children to learn how to accept their own responsibility. It also helps prevent them from accepting any burden that isn't theirs.

7

Increases Sense of Worthiness

Encouraging our children to select reading materials strengthens their sense of self-worth, good judgment and independence.

Shows Family Support

8

Family roles are redefined and strengthened by the simple acts we do as a family unit. By reading aloud to our children, we show that we support them as they are learning how to read.

9

Encourages Self-Expression

Exposure to reading enables children to better express their thoughts and ideas.

Develops Integrity

10

Reading can help develop a child's values and morality through exposure to good and bad characters, situations and their outcomes.

11 Promotes Self-Respect

Nothing shows respect more than talking with your child, rather than to your child. By spending time reading with your children—not just being an authority figure—you show respect for them as developing human beings. Respect is the foundation of self-worth.

Fosters Independence 12

While reading together with an adult, even the youngest child will begin to feel independent because of the interaction as an equal with a grownup. Our children feel empowered by being a valuable part of the family experience. Independence is one of the greatest attributes a child can develop.

13 Instills a Sense of Mutual Respect (Parent for Child; Child for Parent)

Reading time strengthens the idea that our life experiences merit respect and that our roles as parents are vital to our children's well-being. Similarly, we learn to respect one another's choices.

Teaches Your Child How to Ask for Help 14

Interacting with your child while reading to him or her will naturally lead to questions. This exercise teaches children how to ask for help, and how to give help.

15 Helps You to Better Understand Your Child

Sharing reading choices among family members can be a great way to involve yourself and understand your child's point-of-view.

Shares Adult Point-of-View with Child 16

Alternating reading choices can be a great way to share what you like to read ... and leads to discussions about your viewpoints.

17 Explains How Reading Can be Instructional

No doubt, reading can be a joy, but it is also a necessity for the ability to follow instructions—for example, recipes, manuals, food labels and geographical directions.

Becomes an Educational Tool *18*

In order to complete schooling, we must be able to read text books, manuals, guides ... and understand them.

19 Helps Raise Academic and Social Performance

Being informed of our children's academic strengths and weaknesses through our reading time helps us understand what is going on in their lives.

Looks at World History in Exciting New Ways *20*

Books document history... and history is full of lessons to be learned. By reading, our children can learn from the past.

21 Helps with Habits and Attitudes

Parents can help their children learn to read for the sheer pleasure of reading. Once good reading habits are established, the child will be receptive to reading more complex books, and books with differing viewpoints.

Identifies Interests and Nurtures Them 22

We identify, reinforce and expand our children's interests through the selection of the books we read together.

23 Teaches Spirituality Through Examples

Some stories teach us how to have a loving attitude toward family, friends, strangers and our environment. To many, this is the essence of spirituality.

Creates a Family Culture 24

Culture is an important aspect of family life and is passed down through generations. Our family interactions are the lessons of our culture and create lasting values. If we read with our children, they in turn will become cultural teachers during their own lives.

25 Creates Warm Family Memories

The time you and your children share together now will be remembered for the rest of your lives.

Teaches How to Express Ideas 26

Through reading books, children learn how words are put together to form ideas and stories.

27 Encourages a Variety of Reading Materials

Not all reading has to be school-related. Older children can be read to from news-papers, magazines and books. By reading to them from a variety of sources, they are then encouraged to read from different reading materials when on their own.

Nurtures You (as the Reader) 28

Reading with your child is a loving act. You grow as an individual by giving your time to your child.

29 Redefines Parenthood; Expanding the Parental Role

When we share the reading experience, parents learn that authority is best based on mutual understanding and respect.

Builds Special One-on-One Relationships 30

Especially in large families, reading aloud to a child is a good way to establish a close one-on-one relationship.

31 Allows You to Become an Intellectual Role Model

When we read to our children, we become their intellectual role models. This encourages our children to become role models for their children.

Allows for Better Understanding of Each Other 32

Our children never outgrow the need for our understanding and love. We must find appropriate ways to show it as they mature. Reading together is one way to show our understanding and love for our children.

33 Develops Critical Thinking

Through exposure to books with different points of view, children begin to develop the ability to make carefully considered choices. This is an important step toward critical thinking.

Expands Knowledge and an Appreciation for the Arts 34

Parents can introduce their children to the fine arts through books. It can be beneficial to all children to love and appreciate the arts as part of life.

35 Promotes Healthy Problem Solving

Togetherness promotes the sharing of problems before someone explodes in anger or discontent. Through reading, problems can be explored and resolved.

Helps Face Fears of the Unknown 36

By making the unknown familiar... like going to the dentist for the first time, or facing an operation... there is less fear. Reading helps us face our fears of the unknown.

37 Can Ease a Child's Fears When a New Baby Joins the Family

Reading related books on the subject can help with the child's fears about how he or she will be treated and what to expect when a new baby comes home.

Reduces Overall Family Tension

38

Reading aloud together is a social interaction. If there is tension in the family, social interaction can help make the situation better. Reading a good book can also lead to conversations that relieve tension.

39

Teaches that Individual Differences are Okay

Dealing effectively with differing points-of-view is something that can be learned during the give-and-take of reading discussions.

Creates New Family Ties

40

Family unity can be created from the communication and closeness that results from reading together.

41

Strengthens Old Family Ties

By reading to our children, we help them understand that they are part of a family unit that grows as the family grows.

Curbs Inappropriate Emotions

42

By letting our children interact with us, we let them know they are being heard and that there is no reason to withdraw or overreact.

43 Teaches How to Share Emotional Space

Setting aside time to read to our children creates an emotional space for us to share feelings and thoughts.

Explains Difficult Situations 44

Through reading, we can find new ways to explain difficult concepts such as divorce, illness or death in ways that don't over-whelm our children.

45 Examines Unfamiliar Ideas

Improving a child's reading skills can allow him or her to explore other possibilities and take his or her imagination to distant corners of the world.

Establishes a Family Activity 46

Reading to your child establishes a positive routine for today's on-the-run family. Activities done in concert with reading... drawing pictures, locating places on a map ... make reading more interesting.

47 Encourages Laughing Together

Laughing together can lighten our burdens. Humorous books are a welcome break from our hectic daily lives.

Encourages A Sense of Wonder 48

We should always encourage the child-like qualities of openness and curiosity. Questions like, "Why do the stars fall?" or "Where does the moon go during the day?" should always be encouraged.

49 Shares Wisdom

By expanding our reading list to include the great visionaries of our time, such as Amelia Earhart, Martin Luther King, Jr., and Frank Lloyd Wright, we can share the wealth of information man has gained throughout the years.

Helps Them Imagine Their "Impossible" Careers 50

As our children learn about career choices, we encourage them to dream their impossible dreams through reading about them. After all, who can say what kind of jobs will exist in outer space?

51 Teaches Family History

Reading books about family events or family history can help our children understand their own family history.

52 Teaches How Career Choices are Made

Exploring career choices through reading allows children to see a variety of roles, situations and possibilities for themselves.

53 Increases Quality Time Together

There is nothing old-fashioned about sitting close to our children and enjoying quality time together.

Teaches Teamwork 54

Reading together and solving problems gives our children an early start in developing the skills of teamwork, which is the first indicator of success in school.

55 Develops the Ability to Read Alone

By reading to your child, you teach your child the skills necessary to read alone. The more you read to them and demonstrate your love of reading, the more likely they'll become avid readers themselves.

Helps Develop Decision-Making Skills 56

We all need to see the "what ifs" in life, and that there are no decisions without consequences. Reading Aesop's Fables is a good example of aiding decision-making skills.

57 Helps Understand Cultural Differences

Reading opens up a whole world of experiences. Even if we never venture from our own hometown or country, we can visit any place in the world we desire by reading about it.

Teaches How to Focus 58

A fundamental skill of learning is how to focus. Shared reading time is all about focusing on the story being read, and listening for important information. Learning to focus on important information helps our children focus in everyday life.

59 — Improves Homework

Positive interaction from shared reading time can help ease the difficulties that may arise with homework. By sharing reading time, we enable our children to openly ask questions. This can help improve their results on homework and on exams.

Creates a Work Ethic — 60

By expressing our expectations for achievement and responding to our child's reading initiatives and interests, we can create a positive work ethic.

61 — Improves Writing Skills

Proficient readers usually become good writers. Reading encourages self-expression, which enhances one's writing skills.

Improves Performance in School

62

Learning should be a lifelong activity first modeled at home. Studies indicate that success in school can be predicted by a child's third-grade reading scores on achievement tests.

63

Increases Vocabulary Through Exposure to New Words

Children understand several hundred words when they first start school, but they may only be able to read a few dozen. By reading books to your children, you introduce them to an entire world of new words.

Exposes Listener to Good Grammar 64

The more a child is exposed to the written word and grammatically correct sentences, the more likely he or she will use words correctly in the future.

65 Trains the Child in Proper Pronunciation (and Phonics)

Besides expanding a child's vocabulary, reading aloud teaches the proper pronunciation of words.

Stretches the Attention Span and Memory

66

By asking your child to describe what was just read, we are training the mind to remember things.

67

Encourages Curiosity

By reading to our children, we can become a major contributor to their sense of wonder. A child's curiosity is sparked by what is heard, seen and experienced.

Enhances Listening Skills

68

Parents can direct their children's attention when it starts to wander by reading aloud to them and by asking them to repeat what was just read.

69 Encourages Literacy

Literacy is the ability to understand the value of language and its written forms. We are encouraging literacy every time we share reading time with our children.

Encourages Educated Speech 70

Exposure to language that is vastly different from normal television fare can put the child on the path to educated speech. Hollywood's version of speech isn't necessarily grammatically correct.

71   Gives Pre-schoolers a Head Start

Reading to our children, even before they can read themselves, gives them a head start when they begin school. Begin by reading nursery rhymes, Mother Goose stories and poems.

Encourages Self-Expression   72

Encouraging children to participate in a shared reading experience improves an important personal skill: the ability to independently express thoughts.

73   Teaches Children to be Nurturing Parents

Reading aloud to your children is nurturing. Nurturing your child sets an example of how your children should nurture their own children in the future.

Teaches How to
Learn from Mistakes   **74**

Children who make mistakes need to understand that they are still loved. This helps
them learn how to discuss their mistakes
with their parents, teachers and peers.

75 Introduces the Child to
the Richly Textured Lives
of Different People

Books introduce children to the lives of
people far beyond their comprehension: for
example, the lives of the rich and famous,
or the lives of people who live on rice farms
in Asia .

Stimulates the Imagination

76

Reading stimulates the imagination and encourages children to create scenes and visions in their minds. Through reading, children have the opportunity to travel in their minds to any corner of the world.

77

Creates Intellectual Challenges

When we read to our children, we challenge them to understand new concepts, which encourages questions and critical thinking.

Stimulates a World View of Ethnic Diversity

78

Reading books about foreign lands expands a child's understanding of differences in people throughout the world.

79 Exposes a Child to Current Affairs

Reading newspapers and magazines exposes a child to news at home and around the world.

Develops an Appreciation of the Written Word 80

By actually reading themselves or encouraging their children to read, parents and children can develop an appreciation for the written word.

81 Creates a Sense of Belonging

Children should feel like a vital part of the family. Spending time reading to our children helps them understand and accept the difficulties of development. Feeling accepted gives them the insight to create healthier circles of friends, work companions and mates.

82 Helps the Child Distinguish Between Fact and Fiction

At a very young age, children have a hard time realizing that characters in story books are not real. With shared reading time, we can begin the process of teaching our children the difference between fact and fiction.

Increases Awareness of the Real World 83

Reading about real-world situations makes children more aware of life's challenges and successes. It also helps them to hold onto their visions of what the world could be, and gives them the ability to work through the reality of the present and the promise of the future. Through reading, they can see their place in the world and their possibilities for success.

84 Improves Infant Motor Skills

Reading to toddlers from a story-board book improves their dexterity and concentration by letting them turn the pages for you.

Can Help Build Long-Distance Relationships 85

Particularly for absentee parents or grandparents, reading to or with a child at a predetermined time over the phone can build a long-distance relationship.

86 Instills a Love of Books

Through our enthusiasm for reading, a child can develop a love for books and a passion to read.

Can Calm or Help a Child Go to Sleep

87

Babies love to listen to the human voice. Bedtime-story-reading can send your young child into dreamland, or it can simply calm him or her down.

88

Makes Vacations More Memorable By Knowing About the Destination

Vacations are much more fun when your children know something about their destination. If you are going to a famous place or city, read about it to your children. Let them keep a journal of what they see and experience. They can also draw maps of places they've visited.

Exposes a Child to New Information

89

A toddler's world is largely confined to preschool and home. Books open a child's mind to libraries filled with stories about new things . . . new cultures . . . and the universe.

90

Encourages Good Judgment

Judgment is taught through many instances of 'what if.' When we engage our children's minds through reading, we encourage them to recognize what they need to know to make good judgments.

Helps Create a Positive Lifestyle   91

Our daily activity is a life-long lesson. All we do, as well as that which we don't do, becomes part of the fabric of our children's lives. Our conscious choice to spend quality time with our children will have a positive effect on our lives and theirs.

92   Helps Children Mature

By reading to our children, we expose them to life's experiences. This helps a child understand life's situations and helps them mature.

Encourages Positive Attitudes   93

Your positive, helpful behavior is communicated to your child when reading to him or her. The child feels loved and worthy of your attention.

94   Encourages Healthy Compromises

Compromise is not the same as giving in, or just being nice. Healthy compromise is achieved when all people involved in the issue have been heard, valued and considered. Our conversations with our children during shared reading time often address the issues common to them.

Teaches the Meaning of Commitment   95

When our children see our commitment to them through reading every day, they will be more likely to commit themselves to family and personal goals from a young age.

96   Helps Prepare for Life's Challenges

Reading about life's situations in books can give our children the safe distance needed to ask the questions that are on their minds. By spending quality time with them, we can offer guidance, explanations and suggestions while allowing them to think and make judgments. Through this exchange, they develop a better understanding of life.

Trains Children to Speak Clearly   97

Oftentimes, we must pay close attention to what our children are trying to say. While their vocabulary may be limited, their feelings and ideas are vast. As we read to them, we are training them to speak more clearly... and training ourselves to hear their messages.

98 Teaches the Relationship Between Letters & Words

While reading, you can teach your young child to spell a few special words, such as his or her name ... stop or go. By drawing attention to these frequently occurring words, the child begins to understand how letters form words.

Teaches the Appreciation of Life 99

We are surrounded by the everyday miracles and mysteries of life. The more we try to understand mysteries, like the mystery of birth, the more conscious we become of our roles in the world. Through reading, our children can learn about life's many mysteries.

100

Teaches
Tolerance

By taking time to patiently read to our children, we are teaching patience and tolerance.

Teaches
Leadership

101

The skills to be a leader are varied. But a primary factor in leadership is the ability to interact with others while expressing and listening to many points of view to reach a goal. Children do not become leaders overnight. Reading about other leaders helps them realize that they need time to mature and that they'll make mistakes. In short, children need involved parents to help them gain knowledge, use it, assess it and form a life plan that will help ensure their personal and public success.

Evidence-Based Reading

It is evident that times of shared reading are a healthy part of a child's early development, but even the best parents have long days and tight schedules. Sometimes, it's all we can do to make sure the kids have their teeth brushed and ears scrubbed before bedtime, much less spend 30 minutes reading through a book that we'll no doubt revisit three times that week. It can be helpful, then, to be reminded of some of the more quantifiable evidence for the benefits of reading aloud with our children. A quick overview of recent findings in the field of evidence-based reading instruction might coax the work-weary parent to find room in the evening for "just one more page."

There is an undeniably positive correlation between early shared reading experiences and a child's emergent literary ability (the skills or knowledge that children develop before learning the more conventional skills of reading and writing). In shared reading, rudimentary mechanics like learning to hold a book correctly or locating the beginning and ending of the book converge with more subtle understandings like the ability of print to represent the spoken word. Reading aloud also bolsters children's proclivity towards oral language skills, enhances comprehension and memory, and endows children with critical problem-solving abilities that they will need later in life. Children who benefit from regular shared reading times often come away from the experience with an appreciation for reading; an appreciation they take with them into the classroom. This cycle can become a promising force for the young student's intellectual life; in short, reading is habitual. And getting a child "addicted" to reading can be as simple as rethinking the bedtime routine with your young ones.

The evidence for the benefits of shared reading also informs the more practical question of "how." What is the best method for shared reading? Here, the objective evidence drifts into the subjective realm; the method of reading depends, in large part, on the child. What does he like? What interests her? It is paramount for parents to keep the personal interest of their child in mind when attempting to acquaint him or her with the love of reading. Choose age-appropriate books with quality artwork for the child to enjoy. Make sure your child is able to recognize some of the experiences of the characters as experiences they are having in school and free time. Allow room for synthesis ("He's going to the park like we did!") and leave more time than you think for conversation. Whether your child wants to discuss the pictures between the paragraphs or possible motives of the heroine, talk is good. Encourage predictions. Explore new words as you come across them, and consider incorporating a variety of children's literature—no sense in staying in the same culture every night!

With regular times of enjoyable, interesting shared reading, your child should begin to look forward to opening a book as an adventure as opposed to a chore. The skills developing in your daughter or son's eager mind will sprout as they begin to realize that the world around them is beginning to look suspiciously like the stories that mommy and daddy read to them before bed.

We are particularly indebted to two organizations for their commitment to studying the scientific connections between times of shared book-reading and healthy child development. Both The **International Reading Association** and **Reach Out and Read** strive to promote healthy reading habits through raising awareness of the scientific benefits of reading aloud with children.

www.reading.org

www.reachoutandread.org

2013 "Choices" Reading Lists

Below, you will find three distinct lists that have been compiled and organized by the International Reading Association. Each year, thousands of children, young adults, teachers, and librarians around the United States select their favorite recently published books for the "Choices" reading lists. These lists are used in classrooms, libraries, and homes to help young readers find books they will enjoy. We are pleased to present them as they appear on IRA's website in hopes that you will find interesting new material to read with your child.

* denotes books that have received the highest Children's Choice team votes

Children's Choice

A reading list with a twist! Children themselves evaluate the books and write reviews of their favorites. Since 1974, Children's Choices have been a trusted source of book recommendations used by teachers, librarians, parents—and children themselves.

Primary Readers

(K-2)

Amelia Bedelia's First Vote
Herman Parish. Ill. Lynne Avril. HarperCollins Children's Books/Greenwillow.

It's election time, and Amelia decides students should be allowed to vote on rules at school. Amelia's humor and mishaps mixes with valid information about the election process.

Back to Front and Upside Down
Claire Alexander. Eerdmans Books for Young Readers.

Stan loves to draw pictures but when he writes, the letters look wrong. He asks the teacher for help, and letters make sense. The warm story reminds everyone that sometimes we all need help to learn something new.

Bad Apple: A Tale of Friendship
Edward Hemingway. Penguin Young Readers Group.

Mac and Will are unlikely friends. Mac is an apple, and Will is a worm. When the other apples make fun of Mac, Will decides Mac will be happier without him. Will true friendship survive?

Bailey at the Museum
Harry Bliss. Scholastic.

Bailey goes on a field trip to the Museum of Natural History. He likes the dinosaur bones best but quickly learns they aren't for climbing or chewing! Through Bailey's eyes, children get a glimpse of famous exhibits in the museum.

Bedtime for Monsters
Ed Vere. Henry Holt Books for Young Readers.

As a monster "bump bumpity bumps" through the forest and "gloop, gloop, schloops" through the swamp, suspense and tension build. Playful language captivates children as the monster draws nearer, and a silly, surprise ending leaves them relieved and laughing!

*Big Mean Mike
Michelle Knudsen. Ill. Scott Magoon. Candlewick.

Big Mean Mike is the meanest dog around. Big Mean Mike drives a Big Mean car or he did until the cute, fuzzy bunnies show up. Maybe Big Mean Mike isn't quite as gruff as he pretends.

*The Duckling Gets a Cookie!?
Mo Willems. Hyperion Books for Children.

Pigeon feels he's been treated unfairly—AGAIN! When the duckling gets a cookie just by politely asking for it, Pigeon is outraged! The expressions and body language captured in the text and illustrations keep readers young and old laughing hysterically!

Every Cowgirl Loves a Rodeo
Rebecca Janni. Ill. Lynne Avril. Dial Books for Young Readers.

Nellie Sue enters the bike rodeo at the county fair and finds herself roping a goat to help a friend. She might not win a blue ribbon, but her actions remind readers about what's most important in competition and friendship.

The Fly Flew In
David Catrow. Holiday House.

Buzz! The pesky fly flies and disrupts everything. He lands in hair and on food and buzzes around the musicians. Children will keep reading the hilarious antics of swatting and cymbals clashing to get rid of the fly.

Frog and Fly: Six Slurpy Stories
Jeff Mack. Philomel.

Six spare, slurpy stories about frog and fly. Casualties: five flies and one frog. Children will enjoy the cute illustrations that complement their banter and shenanigans.

Goldilocks and the Three Dinosaurs
Mo Willems. HarperCollins Children's Books.

What an amazing new twist on the familiar classic! When three hungry dinosaurs set a trap for Goldilocks, she narrowly escapes. Willems misses no opportunity to amuse the reader with clever text and illustrations that only get funnier with each reread.

Good News, Bad News
Jeff Mack. Chronicle.

A rabbit and mouse go for an eventful picnic with good and bad things happening. Good News and Bad News as the book's only words tell about each superbly illustrated full-page picture. This book is excellent for emergent readers.

I Know a Wee Piggy
Kim Norman. Ill. Henry Cole. Dial Books for Young Readers.

Color-filled read-aloud with a rampaging pig. Children will enjoy piggy's antics and anticipate the chance to predict the next color he runs amuck in.

*I'll Save You Bobo!
Eileen Rosenthal. Ill. Marc Rosenthal. Simon & Schuster.

Willy's own written story comes to life when Earl, his cat, becomes an acting character. Commonalities are noted when roles are reversed with a happy ending. This simple story will stimulate anyone's imagination and desire to write.

Ladybug Girl and Bingo
Jacky Davis. Ill. David Soman. Dial Books for Young Readers.

Lulu and her dog, Bingo, go camping with her family for the first time. When Bingo gets lost in the woods, it's Ladybug Girl to the rescue.

Lenore Finds a Friend: A True Story From Bedlam Farm
Jon Katz. Henry Holt Books for Young Readers.

This true story about a lonely new puppy on Bedlam Farm named Lenore who is finally welcomed by a grumpy ram named Brutus gives children confidence that new friendships can develop when least expected. Irresistible photographs tug at readers' heartstrings.

Library Mouse: A Museum Adventure
Daniel Kirk. Abrams Books for Young Readers.

In this continuation of the story of Sam, the library mouse, he leaves the walls of the library and ventures to the museum. Sam records his adventure in his explorer's journal.

Little Dog Lost: The True Story of a Brave Dog Named Baltic
Mônica Carnesi. Nancy Paulsen Books.

Meet Baltic, a curious dog who suddenly becomes stranded on a sheet of ice as it moves swiftly down the Vistula River in Poland. Read the true story of his dramatic rescue in the icy waters of the Baltic Sea. It is a must read, especially if you love animals!

Llama Llama Time to Share
Anna Dewdney. Viking Children's Books.

Learning to share is difficult. Llama learns to share with a friend after a cherished toy is torn and repaired. Animal characters and few words on a page make the book motivating and meaningful for any reader.

Mice on Ice
Rebecca Emberley and Ed Emberley. Holiday House.

Skate your way into this story of several mice who find themselves carving out a design in the ice. "What is that?" they ask and, instantly, the design takes shape into a creature often feared by mice. Children can find out what it is when you read Mice on Ice.

Miss Fox's Class Gets It Wrong
Eileen Spinelli. Ill. Anne Kennedy. Albert Whitman & Company.

Miss Fox's first-grade students don't understand what is wrong with their teacher. Did she break the law and get into trouble? They make guesses and tell stories. In another Miss Fox story, children will learn a lesson: Don't gossip!

*Nighttime Ninja
Barbara DaCosta. Ill. Ed Young. Little, Brown Books for Young Readers.

While everyone sleeps, the Nighttime Ninja stealthily moves through the quiet house. He is on a secret mission. Children will delight following the little Ninja as he creeps and clambers through the house to find his treasure.

Otto the Book Bear
Katie Cleminson. Disney/Hyperion.

Otto walks out of his book and wanders around the family's house unnoticed. When the family packs away the book without him in it, he goes on an adventure that will leave readers reimagining how books can come alive.

*Pete the Cat and His Four Groovy Buttons
Eric Litwin. Ill. James Dean. HarperCollins Children's Books.

Everyone's favorite cool cat is back, this time wearing a shirt with four groovy buttons. Alas, the buttons pop off one by one and are lost. Will Pete cry? "Goodness, no!" children respond along with the narrator.

Pig Has a Plan
Ethan Long. Holiday House.

Pig plans to take a nap. He can't figure out why everyone else is being so noisy. He tries to escape, only to find a surprise waiting for him. Children will laugh at the surprise ending to Pig's napping plans.

Piggy Bunny
Rachel Vail. Ill. Jeremy Tankard. Feiwel & Friends.

Poor Liam wants to be the Easter Bunny, but he's a pig. He has big dreams and will work hard to reach them. This warm story will show children that with work, dreams can come true.

Plant a Kiss
Amy Krouse Rosenthal. Ill. Peter H. Reynolds. HarperCollins Children's Books.

Dazzling, glittered illustrations, coupled with simple but powerful rhyme capture the fantastic journey of "Little Miss" who "planted a kiss," carefully tended it, believed in its potential to grow, and kindly shared the love she had cultivated throughout the world.

Rat and Roach: Friends to the End
David Covel. Viking Children's Books.

In this comical story, messy Rat and tidy Roach find that friendship between opposites can be a good thing. Simple but well-executed illustrations accentuate their differences and heighten the humor.

Secret Agent Splat!
Rob Scotton. HarperCollins Children's Books.

When Splat the Cat notices someone has messed with his treasured toy ducks, he uses his trusty spy kit to thoroughly investigate. The culprit's motive comes as a surprise! Clever duck code letters present readers with their own puzzle-solving opportunity!

Señorita Gordita
Helen Ketteman. Ill. Will Terry. Albert Whitman & Company.

This Tex-Mex flavored retelling of The Gingerbread Man is rich with cultural references as hungry animals of the southwest chase Señorita Gordita through the desert. A glossary of Spanish words and a recipe for gorditas provide the perfect finishing touch!

Silly Doggy!
Adam Stower. Orchard/Scholastic.

Newspaper clippings alerting the public of escaped zoo animals start this whimsical tale. Confusing a big, brown, hairy, four-legged animal with a tail and wet nose for a dog, Lily's amusing, beautifully illustrated adventures with an escaped bear unfold!

The Three Ninja Pigs
Corey Rosen Schwartz. Ill. Dan Santat. Penguin Young Readers Group.

A comical, rhythmic mix of martial arts meets fairy tale. When the three little pigs are tired of being bullied by the big, bad wolf they decide to learn to defend themselves. This hilarious story can teach lessons about bullying, perseverance, and confidence.

Tyler Makes Pancakes!
Tyler Florence. Ill. Craig Frazier. HarperCollins Children's Books.

Tyler dreams about pancakes. In the morning, he decides to surprise his parents by making some. The friendly grocer tells him where each ingredient comes from. Tyler's dog, Tofu, tags along on this adventure. The blueberry pancake recipe is included.

Young Readers

(Grades 3-4)

5,000 Awesome Facts (About Everything!)
National Geographic Kids. Ill. with photographs. National Geographic Children's Books.

This book has something for everyone, including reluctant readers! Each cleverly titled two-page spread offers facts organized around a variety of subjects, such as "100 Shark Facts You Can Sink Your Teeth Into!" Includes an index for easy navigation.

Aaron Rodgers and the Green Bay Packers: Super Bowl XLV
Michael Sandler. Ill. with photographs. Bearport.

Aaron Rodgers replaced the idolized quarterback Brett Favre. He had proved he was a good player, helping the team win important games. Rodgers, however, would need to lead the team to win a Super Bowl game.

Another Brother
Matthew Cordell. Feiwel & Friends.

Davey is an only child who relishes being the center of attention. Then one day his mom has a baby brother, then another and another and...soon, Davey is one of 12! Read how Davey deals with his brothers and find out the new surprise waiting for him!

*Bad Kitty for President
Nick Bruel. Roaring Brook.

Kids learn the language and logistics of elections through Bad Kitty's campaign for the presidency of the Neighborhood Cat Club. Bad Kitty's signature antics and Nick Bruel's blend of text and illustrations keep kids laughing. Includes a glossary of election terms.

Bully
Patricia Polacco. Penguin Young Readers Group.

Everything is going perfectly for Lyla in her new school until she stands up against a popular group of girls. She becomes the girls' next target. This great story will help young people explore the issue of bullying in cyberspace and on social networks.

Dear Cinderella
Mary Jane Kensington and Marian Moore. Ill. Julie Olson. Orchard/Scholastic.

This book is a twist on traditional fairy tales. It is a collection of letters between Cinderella and Snow White. They share their stories of wicked stepmothers and dreamy princes.

Dolphins in the Navy
Meish Goldish. Ill. with photographs. Bearport.

Dolphins have been trained by the U.S. Navy to do important and dangerous jobs. They find bombs and look for enemies. This book tells how the Navy trained and cared for both dolphins and sea lions.

Freaky-Strange Buildings
Michael Sandler. Ill. with photographs. Bearport.

Students eagerly hop aboard for an exciting tour of the world's most unusual buildings. Comparisons such as "about as tall as 30 giraffes stacked on top of each other" assist readers in understanding buildings' unique features. Index and glossary included.

Garmann's Secret
Stian Hole. Eerdmans Books for Young Readers.

Even though the twins, Hannah and Johanna, look identical, Garmann knows they're actually very different. One day Johanna takes Garmann to their secret place in the woods, and the two of them share their own secrets and an adventure together.

*Get the Scoop on Animal Poop! From Lions to Tapeworms: 251 Cool Facts About Scat, Frass, Dung, and More!
Dawn Cusick. Ill. with photographs. Imagine.

Kids who pick up this book for gross-out value will stick around for the bright photo illustrations and fascinating facts. Includes a glossary, further resources, and two indexes (subject and organism).

Giants Beware!
Jorge Aguirre. Ill. Rafael Rosado. First Second.

Feisty Claudette, her cowardly brother, and a princess wannabe are on an action-filled and often funny quest to slay giants. In this graphic novel, they learn that being a hero takes intelligence, courage, and heart.

Great Dane: Gentle Giant
Stephen Person. Ill. with photographs. Bearport.

Gibson is a therapy dog, and he was the tallest Great Dane in the Guinness Book of Records. Then George stood even taller than Gibson! Children will enjoy reading fun facts about the gentle and tallest dogs in the world.

*Homer
Diane deGroat and Shelley Rotner. Orchard/ Scholastic.

Will Homer, the hard-hitting Golden Retriever, help the Doggers triumph over the Hounds? Older children can't wait to read which team wins the dog championship in this delightfully fun baseball story.

Illusionology: The Secret Science of Magic
Albert Schafer. Ill. David Wyatt and Levi Pinfold. Candlewick.

Enter the fascinating world of magicians and their illusions. Learn the secrets of the great masters and perform your own tricks with step-by-step instructions in this book full of flaps, envelopes, and magician tools.

Judy Moody and the Bad Luck Charm
Megan McDonald. Ill. Peter H. Reynolds. Candlewick.

Judy Moody's spunky personality continues to fascinate 8- and 9-year-old readers with familiar events to which they can relate. In this fast-paced adventure, Judy Moody's lucky penny initially brings her abundant good fortune, but good luck can't last forever!

*Just Joking: 300 Hilarious Jokes, Tricky Tongue Twisters, and Ridiculous Riddles
National Geographic Children's Books. Ill. with photographs. National Geographic Children's Books.

This hilarious joke book is loaded with full-color and eye-catching photos. Kids enjoy challenging one another with tongue twisters and were entertained by the jokes, which often feature animals and are accompanied by bold graphics. Captions next to many of the photos inform readers with interesting facts about wild animals.

Kevin Durant
Michael Sandler. Ill. with photographs. Bearport.

Short biography about NBA star Kevin Durant focuses on his hard work, on-the-court success, and charitable   contributions. A glossary with key vocabulary makes this a useful learning tool as well as a motivating sports book.

Knuckle & Potty Destroy Happy World
James Proimos. Christy Ottaviano Books.
Tiger and Bear, aka Knuckle and Potty, are fed up with their cute and cuddly image and go on a mission to convince their so-called "creators" to toughen up their act. What follows is a goofy and laugh-out-loud story that combines graphic novel cartooning and first-person narrative.

Last Laughs: Animal Epitaphs
J. Patrick Lewis and Jane Yolen. Ill. Jeffrey Stewart Timmins. Charlesbridge.

This collection of animal epitaphs is witty and full of puns. Included are tributes to the chicken who didn't quite make it across the road and the deer who becomes venison, among others.

Looking at Lincoln
Maira Kalman. Nancy Paulsen Books.

Older children will trace Lincoln's journey from a log cabin to the presidency. Fun-filled facts help children get a close and personal view of Abraham Lincoln. They will learn about his favorite foods and music and his battle against slavery.

Max Goes to the Moon: A Science Adventure With Max the Dog
Jeffrey Bennett. Ill. Alan Okamoto. Big Kid Science.

Max, the dog, and Tori, his human friend, pave the way for the return to space travel and to a space station on the moon. This adventurous story is combined with boxes filled with the science behind the story.

The Monster Returns
Peter McCarty. Henry Holt Books for Young Readers.

When a paper airplane flies in his window, Jeremy finds out his monster is returning. Jeremy must think quickly. He invites his friends to help him with his plan.

My Pop-Up World Atlas
Anita Ganeri. Ill. Stephen Waterhouse. Templar.

The authors make geography come alive. Interesting facts, colorful illustrations, and multilayered continental pop-ups will keep children searching for more geographical facts about their world.

Pigmares: Porcine Poems of the Silver Screen
Doug Cushman. Charlesbridge.

A little piggy watches scary monster movies before bedtime and has nightmares, or "pigmares." Seventeen clever Pig poems spin off of famous creepy classic movies.

*Pluto Visits Earth!
Steve Metzger. Ill. Jared D. Lee. Orchard/ Scholastic.

Disgruntled at being downgraded by astronomers to a dwarf planet in 2006, Pluto visits Earth to regain his status. While on Earth, a young boy helps Pluto realize that size doesn't matter. Big or small, you can be equally special!

Quiz Whiz: 1,000 Super Fun, Mind- Bending, Totally Awesome Trivia Questions
National Geographic Kids. Ill. with photographs. National Geographic Children's Books.

Children will have a blast with this jam-packed trivia quiz book. Readers are presented with 1,000 questions on topics that include history, science, math, geography, and pop culture. A fun book to keep the mind informed and entertained.

Saving Animals After Tornadoes
Stephen Person. Ill. with photographs. Bearport.

This book chronicles heartwarming stories of several animals whose lives were threatened by tornadoes. Children who enjoyed this book will undoubtedly be intrigued by other titles in this series that consider animals' fates when faced with fire, floods, and volcanoes.

Stupendous Sports Stadiums
Michael Sandler. Ill. with photographs. Bearport.

Part of a series that also examines amusement park rides, buildings, and skyscrapers. Eight sports stadiums are identified by their opening date, location, capacity, and stupendous feature. A table of contents, captions, glossary, and index aid in navigation of text.

Surviving the Hindenburg
Larry Verstraete. Ill. David Geister. Sleeping Bear.

A sudden explosion and roaring fire surround Werner, and the 14-year-old cabin boy must find an escape. The nonfiction story gives a gripping account of one person's survival from the fiery furnace of the historical Hindenburg disaster.

Third Grade Angels
Jerry Spinelli. Arthur Levine Books/Scholastic.

A third-grade teacher awards her best children with angel halos. George changes his attitude, expresses his thoughts, and works hard to become an angel. Although it appears that he will not get it, an unexpected event brings victory.

Touch the Sky: Alice Coachman, Olympic High Jumper
Ann Malaspina. Ill. Eric Velasquez. Albert Whitman & Company.

Inspiring and beautifully illustrated. Alice Coachman grows up in 1930s rural Georgia dreaming of being a high jumper. She is eventually added to the Tuskegee Institute track team and becomes the first black woman to win an Olympic gold medal.

Advanced Readers

(Grades 5-6)

A Black Hole Is Not a Hole
Carolyn Cinami DeCristofano. Ill. Michael Carroll. Charlesbridge.

Interesting information and detailed pictures draw older children into the scientific exploration of black holes in outer space. Older readers will keep turning the page to find out facts about the dark mystery in the universe.

The Boy Project: Notes and Observations of Kara McAllister
Kami Kinard. Scholastic.

Boyfriend-obsessed Kara is the only girl in school who doesn't have one. She decides to apply the scientific method to this problem—studying boys, taking notes, and graphing observations. Hypothesis: Readers will laugh and cringe as Kara's experiment backfires.

Broxo
Zack Giallongo. First Second.

Princess Zora sets out alone into the dark forest. She encounters the young warrior Broxo and together they fight through many dangers to discover the mystery of the Peryton clan. Nonstop action and boy-meets-girl backdrop propel the graphic novel.

Cardboard
Doug Tennapel. Graphix/Scholastic.

A lonely father and son create cardboard real-life characters with a magic machine. A war between good and bad characters is fought with their involvement. Comic strip reading creates high interest for both readers and nonreaders.

Dark Mansions
Dinah Williams. Ill. with photographs. Bearport.

This nonfiction text profiles several famous "haunted" mansions and the lore surrounding them. The stories are supported with photographs, sidebars, and an extensive glossary that helps provide context.

*Dork Diaries 4: Tales From a Not-So- Graceful Ice Princess
Rachel Renée Russell. Simon & Schuster.

Written in quickly read, illustrated diary entries, adolescent girls resonate with the issues Nikki faces. As she works to save the animal shelter from closing, she must also deal with mean girl MacKenzie, her crush Brandon, self-doubt, and her totally embarrassing family.

Freaky Fast Frankie Joe
Lutricia Clifton. Holiday House.

With mom in jail, Frankie moves in with his father, stepmother, and four half-brothers. While managing his "Freaky Fast Delivery Service," designed to raise money so he can reunite with his mother, Frankie gains a new understanding of life.

Goosebumps: Wanted: The Haunted Mask
R.L. Stine. Goosebumps/Scholastic.

In this Halloween tale, an evil, ugly mask does much more than scare people at a party. The mask turns an ordinary Halloween party into a horribly haunted affair.

Hades: Lord of the Dead (Olympians, Vol. 4)
George O'Connor. First Second.

Hades, the Lord of the Underworld, rises up to star in this action-packed tale of love and revenge. Not only is the story an exciting retelling of Hades's abduction of Persephone, but also the art offers breathtakingly beautiful renditions of the underworld and other mythical locations.

Haunted Caves
Natalie Lunis. Ill. with photographs. Bearport.

Haunted Caves takes readers inside 11 of the most frightening, claustrophobia-inducing places on Earth. From a lost treasure in Spain to a giant underground lake in the United States, you'll see it all in startling, full-color detail!

Haunted Histories: Creepy Castles, Dark Dungeons, and Powerful Palaces
J.H. Everett and Marilyn Scott-Waters. Christy Ottaviano Books.

The Ancient Order of Ghostorians visit ghosts and gather historical information. They provide children with a fun and interesting look at castles, medieval class systems, dungeons and prisons, torture, workhouses, palaces from England to India, and heraldic symbols and monuments.

The Hero's Guide to Saving Your Kingdom
Christopher Healy. Ill. Todd Harris. Walden Pond/ HarperCollins Children's Books.

Four rejected princes, who in the past have only been known collectively as "Prince Charming," stumble upon an evil plan that threatens their kingdoms.

Thwarting several evils, heroism is finally acknowledged! This original fractured fairy tale has cross-gender appeal.

Horrible Hauntings: An Augmented Reality Collection of Ghosts and Ghouls
Shirin Yim Bridges. Ill. William Maughan. Goosebottom.

Eight ghost sightings are described and coupled with eight full-page complementary illustrations. After uploading a free app to their phone or tablet, students worked to see ghosts come to life in these illustrations. This motivated even the most reluctant reader!

I Lay My Stitches Down: Poems of American Slavery
Cynthia Grady. Ill. Michele Wood. Eerdmans Books for Young Readers.

Each rich and detailed poem is part of a quilting pattern design weaving together the hopes, dreams, and spirituality of American slaves. Rich in symbolism, older readers will appreciate the beauty of each story told in poetic form.

Legends of Zita the Spacegirl
Ben Hatke. First Second.

In this graphic novel, Zita has a robot double that is making trouble. Zita is determined to find a way to return home to Earth. Her adventure helps her learn how to be herself.

*Liar & Spy
Rebecca Stead. Wendy Lamb Books.

When seventh grader Georges moves into a Brooklyn apartment building, he meets Safer, a 12-year-old self-proclaimed spy. Safer convinces Georges to be his first spy recruit and together they watch Mr. X, a neighbor who might be hiding a dangerous secret. Readers won't be able to put this one down!

*Pickle: The (Formerly) Anonymous Prank Club of Fountain Point Middle School
Kim Baker. Ill. Tim Probert. Roaring Brook.

Ben Diaz and four engaging middle grades characters from various ethnic backgrounds form the League of Pickle Masters, a secret society for goofing off and performing harmless pranks. This book keeps students laughing while learning valuable lessons about friendship.

Pip and the Wood Witch Curse: A Spindlewood Tale (Book 1)
Chris Mould. Albert Whitman & Company.

Pip runs away from the orphanage and from being a pirate's cabin boy. He comes to Hangman's Hollow and the city's war with the forest and the wood witches. This dark tale is the first in the new Spindlewood Tales series.

Presidential Pets: The Weird, Wacky, Little, Big, Scary, Strange Animals That Have Lived in the White House
Julia Moberg. Ill. Jeff Albrecht Studios. Imagine.

Poetry, presidential stats, and interesting pets fill this colorfully illustrated book. Discovering that the White House was home to pets such as a dog named Satan, bear cubs, alligators, and a swearing parrot provides children with a fun way to learn presidential facts.

*Rebel McKenzie
Candice Ransom. Disney/Hyperion.

Rebel wants to attend the Ice Age Kids' Dig and Safari, a summer camp, but summer camps cost money. Rebel sets out to win a beauty contest and some prize money, but ends up learning a lot about herself.

Remarkable
Lizzie K. Foley. Dial Books for Young Readers.

Ordinary Jane Doe does not fit in with others in the town of Remarkable, where everyone is extraordinary. When citizens in town are in jeopardy of having damaging secrets divulged, Jane must solve the mystery and save the day.

Ruby Redfort Look Into My Eyes
Lauren Child. Candlewick.

Ruby is a super-genius 13-year-old spy who cracks codes and goes onto daring missions with her loyal butler, Hitch. She goes after a crime organization, but one thing gets her into trouble: She can't keep a secret.

Same Sun Here
Silas House and Neela Vaswani. Ill. Hilary Schenker. Candlewick.

In this novel written in two voices, the son of a Kentucky coal miner and an Indian immigrant girl in New York City find they have much in common. Their friendship creates a bridge between their cultural differences.

Shadow
Michael Morpurgo. Feiwel & Friends.

This winner of several awards is the adventurous story of a boy and his mother. They've fled war-torn Afghanistan. Captured and imprisoned, their only hope is a good friend and the need to find a lost loyal dog.

Spider-Man: Inside the World of Your Friendly Neighborhood Hero
Matthew K. Manning, with additional text by Tom DeFalco. DK Publishing.

With fast-paced action, the inside story behind Spider-Man springs to life. Learn how his costume was created. Find out about his friends and how he made enemies. The history of Spider-Man is a true page-turner for older readers.

*Stickman Odyssey, Book 2: The Wrath of Zozimos
Christopher Ford. Philomel.

Another mythological misadventure for the comical Zozimos in this reimagined Odyssey. Fast-paced action and silliness will keep readers attentive and entertained as the stick-figured hero seeks to reclaim the kingdom of Sticatha.

The Takedown of Osama bin Laden
Natalie Lunis. Ill. with photographs. Bearport.

Step-by-step the hunt for America's most wanted Osama bin Laden engrosses older readers. They will follow the search from Afghanistan to Pakistan and read about the bravery of Navy Seals who went on a daring mission.

Today's Air Force Heroes
Miriam Aronin. Ill. with photographs. Bearport.

In these true tales of real heroes, read amazing accounts of courageous men and women who put their lives at risk. This book demonstrates the diversity among the many who have stepped up to make our country safer.

Undead Ed
Rotterly Ghoulstone. Ill. Nigel Baines. Razorbill.

Ed Bagley is on a mission to save his town—from his own evil left arm! The hilariously gory misadventures of a newly undead zombie will have you ROFL. It's gross-out fic with tons of pics.

Unusual Creatures: A Mostly Accurate Account of Some of Earth's Strangest Animals
Michael Hearst. Ill. Arjen Noordeman, Christie Wright, and Jelmer Noordeman. Chronicle.

Older readers will delve in to explore the weird and goofy-looking creatures roaming the earth. Interesting facts, habitats, and scientific names are only part of the most unusual creatures' worlds that will keep readers turning the pages.

Weird But True! 4: 300 Outrageous Facts
National Geographic Kids. Ill. with photographs. National Geographic Children's Books.

Brightly colored, large illustrations with few words tell about unusual and interesting little-known facts throughout the world. Once one starts to read the book, it will be difficult to put it down again.

White House Kids: The Perks, Pleasures, Problems, and Pratfalls of the Presidents' Children
Joe Rhatigan. Ill. Jay Shinn. Imagine.

This is a collection of fun and unusual facts about some of the kids who have had the opportunity to live in the White House. Want to bowl? Just go to the basement! Fascinating tales of real-life kids.

Teacher's Choice

Since 1989, the Teachers' Choices project has developed an annual annotated reading list of new books that will encourage young people to read. These are books that kids will enjoy—and that contribute to learning across the curriculum.

Primary Readers

(K-2)

A Leaf Can Be...
Laura Purdie Salas. Ill. Violeta Dabija. Lerner.

This simple, rhyming text shows readers the many things a leaf can be. Through short noun/verb couplets, young readers have the chance to play with words and build an understanding that leaves are more than tree decorators.

And Then It's Spring
Julie Fogliano. Ill. Erin E. Stead. Macmillan.

It is hard to believe that the cold, brown earth will turn green again. When a young boy plants a seed and waits for it to grow, he holds the belief alive. The rain comes, the world turns green, and then it's spring.

Body Actions
Shelley Rotner. Ill. Shelley Rotner and David A. White. Holiday House.

Photographs with superimposed drawings combine with simple textual explanations to help young readers take an inside look at the body systems and the five senses. Endnotes provide more information for the teacher or advanced reader.

Chopsticks
Amy Krouse Rosenthal. Ill. Scott Magoon. Disney/ Hyperion.

Effective use of chopsticks requires two, which is why one chopstick stays behind with his broken counterpart. When the broken part decides that the other shouldn't sit around, Chopstick ventures out. Although he keeps busy, he realizes that things are always better with his friend.

Creepy Carrots!
Aaron Reynolds. Ill. Peter Brown. Simon & Schuster.

Jasper Rabbit loves carrots and always stops at Crakenhopper Field to get a snack. Soon, he thinks that the carrots are following him, and he builds a fence to keep them in their field. He realizes that he also built a fence to keep himself out, doing the carrots an unexpected favor.

Green
Laura Vaccaro Seeger. Macmillan.

This concept book has outstanding illustrations that show readers the many variations of green. Through the use of die-cut pages, readers learn that green shows up in many shades, from forest to lime, and the objects that represent those are presented throughout the text.

How Many Jelly Beans? A Giant Book of Giant Numbers!
Andrea Menotti. Ill. Yancey Labat. Chronicle.

If you could have as many jelly beans as you wanted, how many would you choose? That question is this book's premise, which begins having readers count by 25s but quickly moves to larger numbers. This illustrations and foldouts provide effective visuals.

Otto the Book Bear
Katie Cleminson. Disney/Hyperion.

When no one is reading Otto's book, he can wander out of it to explore. Otto struggles to find a welcoming place but then stumbles into the library. There he finds other book animals to explore with before returning to his own pages.

Plant a Little Seed
Bonnie Christensen. Macmillan.

This book reviews for young children the growing season for seeds. The characters plant their seeds each spring, water them, and then wait. As they are waiting, readers see bees, butterflies, and the rain, as the plants stretch closer to the sky each day.

Rocket Writes a Story
Tad Hills. Random House.

Since Rocket learned to read, he has been collecting words. Rocket wants to do something with them, so he decides to write a story. Rocket needs a lot of thinking and observing time, but he eventually writes a story and makes a friend.

Intermediate Readers

(Grades 3-5)

The Beetle Book
Steve Jenkins. Houghton Mifflin.

Did you know that one of every four plants or animals on earth is a beetle? This book explores the life cycle and habitats of beetles from around the world. Detailed text provides facts while cut-paper and torn-paper collages provide visual interest.

The Boy Who Harnessed the Wind
William Kamkwamba and Bryan Mealer. Ill. Elizabeth Zunon. Penguin.

Fourteen-year-old William Kamkwamba was determined to help his Malawi village recover from a severe drought that had ravaged the food supply. By reading books and using junk parts, he constructed a windmill to harness the wind and make electricity.

Brothers at Bat: The True Story of an Amazing All-Brother Baseball Team
Audrey Vernick. Ill. Steven Salerno. Clarion.

The Acerra family had 16 children, including 12 baseball-playing brothers. In the 1930s, the boys formed their own semiprofessional team and became the longest playing all-brother baseball team in history.

Dogs on Duty: Soldiers' Best Friends on the Battlefield and Beyond
Dorothy Hinshaw Patent. Bloomsbury Walker.

Military Working Dogs have served alongside soldiers on the battlefield since ancient times. How these dogs are trained and the vital roles they play in all branches of military service are highlighted through text and stunning photographs.

Each Kindness
Jacqueline Woodson. Ill. E.B. Lewis. Penguin.

When a newcomer is shunned by the popular girls, their teacher shows them how small acts of kindness can change the world. It is too late to undo the harm they have caused, but these students—and yours— will take this antibullying message to heart.

I, Too, Am America
Langston Hughes. Ill. Bryan Collier. Simon & Schuster.

Collier showcases the history of the Pullman Porters by lending his artistic interpretation to the famous Langston Hughes poem. Endnotes provide additional information about the contributions of these noble servants.

Rachel Carson and Her Book That Changed the World
Laurie Lawlor. Ill. Laura Beingesser. Holiday House.

Rachel Carson was an ordinary child who grew up to be a pioneer environmentalist. This biography shows that anyone can make a difference. A detailed epilogue explains more about the lasting impact of her book, Silent Spring.

A Rock Is Lively
Dianna Hutts Aston. Ill. Sylvia Long. Chronicle.

Vivid illustrations combine with poetic text to help readers see inside the fascinating world of geology. Detailed explanations extend students' understanding of the form and function of rocks and minerals.

A Strange Place to Call Home: The World's Most Dangerous Habitats & the Animals That Call Them Home
Marilyn Singer. Ill. Ed Young. Chronicle.

Through a variety of poetic forms and collage illustrations, readers will discover 14 creatures that thrive in seemingly uninhabitable locations. Endnotes provide more details about each creature, and explanations of the different types of poems will guide aspiring writers.

Survival at 120 Above
Debbie S. Miller. Ill. Jon Van Zyle. Bloomsbury Walker.

Imagine a world where the daily temperature swings as much as 75 degrees and animals must survive years of drought with little relief. Life in Australia's Simpson Desert is showcased. A glossary of terms supplements the text and illustrations.

Advanced Readers

(Grades 6-8)

Buried Alive! How 33 Miners Survived 69 Days Deep Under the Chilean Desert
Elaine Scott. Clarion.

Photographs, diagrams, and text tell the heartwrenching story of 33 men who were trapped 2,000 feet underground in a desert mine while the world watched and waited. Additional resources provide suggestions for further exploration.

Fire in the Streets
Kekla Magoon. Simon & Schuster.

Chicago in 1968 is a difficult time to be a 14-year-old girl, especially if you hope to join the Black Panthers like your older brother. Maxie finds her identity in spite of the chaos, violence, and injustice that surround her.

Glory Be
Augusta Scattergood. Scholastic.

Gloriana Hemphill always celebrates her Fourth of July birthday at the community pool, but 1964 brings changes that she had not anticipated. Her hometown of Hanging Moss, Mississippi, is in turmoil, and Glory must negotiate her way through changing relationships with family and friends.

Hand in Hand: Ten Black Men Who Changed America
Andrea Davis Pinkney. Ill. Brian Pinkney. Disney/ Hyperion.

This biography profiles the lives of 10 brave men from different eras of American history. Readers will discover that each of these men left an indelible legacy and that courage and determination can turn ordinary citizens into heroes.

Lincoln's Last Days: The Shocking Assassination That Changed America Forever

Bill O'Reilly and Dwight Jon Zimmerman. Henry Holt.

This adaptation of the adult book Killing Lincoln is filled with period photographs, diagrams, and maps detailing the event that changed the course of American history. The back matter provides additional facts, resources, timelines, and websites.

The Lions of Little Rock

Kristin Levine. G.P. Putnam.

A first-person narrator helps readers understand life in Little Rock, Arkansas, in 1958, one year after the integration of Central High School. Twelve-year-old Marlee struggles to understand the changes in her family and her community, especially after her new friend is removed from school.

Somebody, Please Tell Me Who I Am

Harry Mazer and Peter Lerangis. Simon & Schuster.

Everyone is surprised when the popular Ben joins the Army right after high school. His family and friends are even more shocked when they have to deal with the consequences when he returns home after suffering a traumatic brain injury.

Steve Jobs: Thinking Differently

Patricia Lakin. Simon & Schuster.

Everyone knows that Steve Jobs was an entrepreneur and a visionary. This book discusses Jobs's triumphs, but it also lets us see his human side. Readers are reminded that people who dare to dream can change the world.

Titanic: Voices From the Disaster

Deborah Hopkinson. Scholastic.

Archival photographs, telegrams, letters, and first-person accounts from passengers, witnesses, and crew members provide multiple perspectives on the sinking of the Titanic. Nearly 50 pages of endnotes provide additional information and suggestions for further reading.

Wonder

R.J. Palacio. Random House.

Auggie is not like most kids his age, though he desperately wants to be. A severe facial deformity has kept him out of school until fifth grade. A shifting narrator helps readers imagine what it is like to be Auggie or one of his friends or family members.

Young Adults' Choice

Since 1987, the Young Adults' Choices project has developed an annual list of new books that will encourage adolescents to read. The books are selected by the readers themselves, so they are bound to be popular with middle and secondary school students. The reading list is a trusted source of book recommendations, used by adolescents, their parents, teachers, and librarians.

All My Friends Are Still Dead
Avery Monsen and Jory John. Chronicle.

This humorous collection of cartoons and drawings depicts a variety of people and other life forms as they deal with the existential aspects of their lives (and deaths).

Boy21
Matthew Quick. Little, Brown Books for Young Readers.

Finley, an introverted teen, is the only Anglo player on his high school's varsity basketball team. When former basketball phenomenon Russ moves into town after his parents' murder, Finley is asked by his basketball coach to befriend him. Identity, injustice, and loss are explored through this unique friendship.

Breaking Beautiful
Jennifer Shaw Wolf. Walker Childrens.

Following the death of her boyfriend, Trip, in a car accident, Allie is overwhelmed, left scarred, and unable to recall what happened. Crushed by survivor's guilt and loss, Allie is simultaneously relieved to be rid of the abuse Trip imposed. As the suspicious circumstances of the accident are uncovered, Allie must reveal difficult truths.

Cinder
Marissa Meyer. Square Fish.

First in a series of four planned novels (The Lunar Chronicles), this fresh retelling of the classic fairy tale is set in a dystopian future and portrays the heroine as a cyborg mechanic. This fast-paced adventure includes a romantic prince, an evil queen, a deadly plague, and a dysfunctional stepfamily.

City of Lost Souls
Cassandra Clare. Walker Childrens.

The fifth volume in the Mortal Instruments series, this fantasy-adventure-romance features vampires, werewolves, warlocks, faeries, and a teenage love triangle. Clare and the Shadow hunters try to stop her evil brother, Sebastian, but as he is "bound" to her beloved Jace, how can one be killed and not the other?

Cracked
K.M. Walton. Simon Pulse.

This powerful and empathetic picture of bullying is told from the perspectives of abuser and abused. Through alternating narratives, they reveal a tragic history as victims of physical, emotional, and verbal abuse. After becoming roommates in a psych ward, each attempts a dramatic escape from his pain.

Dead to You
Lisa McMann. Simon Pulse.

Ethan is abducted at 7 years old from his front lawn. At 16, he is reunited with his parents. He has no memory of his life before he was taken. His younger brother Blake believes he is not his brother. Mama says the DNA test is not necessary. Is it?

Every Day
David Levithan. Knopf Books for Young Readers.

'A' lives a nomadic life, switching daily from body to body. He refuses to form emotional bonds with others until he meets Rhiannon, who touches his heart. When 'A' reveals his true identity to Rhiannon, she struggles with his constantly changing outward identities. Can love triumph, or is 'A' asking too much?

The Fault in Our Stars
John Green. Dutton Juvenile.

Hazel and Gus, who meet in a Cancer Kid Support Group, decide to take risks as they embark on a life-affirming trip to Amsterdam. During their journey of mutual understanding they find friendship, happiness, and love while facing the injustice of terminal illnesses. Love softens and magnifies the reality and sorrow to come.

Fracture
Megan Miranda. Walker Childrens.

It's cold—really cold—when Delaney falls through the ice. She is under freezing water for 11 minutes but, strangely, she awakens from a coma six days later with no apparent brain damage. Now things are different. Pulled toward death, Delaney tries to find a way to understand her new life.

Getting Over Garrett Delaney
Abby McDonald. Scholastic.

Sadie has been in love with Garrett Delaney for far too long. She finally realizes that no matter how 'perfect' she is for him, Garrett will never see her as more than a friend. Sadie picks up the pieces of her broken heart and moves on in the best possible way.

Girl Meets Boy
Kelly Milner Halls. Chronicle.

This collection of "he said/she said" stories tell of hope and heartbreak as the problems of forming youthful romantic relationship are explored. The complexity and fragility of love relationships are wonderfully constructed. Twelve of the most dynamic and engaging contemporary YA authors are featured in this one-of-a-kind compilation.

Hades
Alexandra Adornetto. Square Fish.

The Halo series continues as angels battle demons, putting the power of love to the test. Despite the care of her archangel siblings and Xavier's love, Beth is tricked into a motorcycle ride ending in Hell. As demon Jack Thorn bargains for her release, Beth and her loved ones may all be destroyed.

If I Lie
Corrine Jackson. Simon Pulse.

Just before Quinn's boyfriend Carey deploys to Afghanistan, Quinn is caught kissing another boy. Shunned, Quinn loses her friends, her reputation, and her identity. The ostracism intensifies after Carey goes missing in action. However, the kiss wasn't really a betrayal; Quinn is keeping a secret. Now she must decide among honor, loyalty, and truth.

The Last Free Cat
Jon Blake. Albert Whitman Teen.

In the future, unregulated cat ownership is illegal, punishable even by death. But when a beautiful, free, calico cat arrives in her yard, Jade can't resist and keeps her. When she confides her secret to her classmate Kris, tragedy ensues and they are forced to take the cat and flee.

The List
Siobhan Vivian. Push.

Every year at Mount Washington High School, an anticipated and dreaded list is posted. On it, eight girls are listed; in each grade, the 'prettiest' and the 'ugliest' are identified. The authorship of the list is anonymous, but the impact of being named is far reaching. Themes of love, friendship, sisterhood, family, and bullying are explored.

The Mark of Athena
Rick Riordan. Hyperion Book CH.

Action, excitement, and adventure reign as the Heroes of Atlantis series continues. Journeying across land and seas in the Argo II to Rome, Percy and his fellow avengers find dangerous surprises, suspenseful discoveries, and unimaginable horrors. This time, our heroes may have met a force and challenge too great.

Monument 14
Emmy Laybourne. Feiwel & Friends.

Set in the near future, this is the story of socially awkward Dean, forced to become a leader when a series of natural disasters erupt. Trapped with 13 kids, Dean and his group must create a refuge to survive in a world gone completely mad.

My Life Next Door
Huntley Fitzpatrick. Dial.

Samantha secretly admires the new, perfect family next door although her mother forbids her to socialize with them. As forbidden relationships develop, Samantha must make tough decisions about love, family, friends, and self. Is it possible to have it all, or will her choices make her lose everything?

The Night She Disappeared
April Henry. Henry Holt.

Kayla has been kidnapped and brutalized while held hostage by a psychopath. With the passing of time, hope fades for Kayla's safe return. When Gabbie and Drew discover Kayla was not the intended victim, they set out to find her. Suspense reigns as they find slender threads of clues that have eluded the police.

October Mourning: A Song for Matthew Shepard
Lesléa Newman. Candlewick.

Poetically depicting Matthew Shepherd's horrific murder in 1998, this powerful work recounts the crime through several points of view, including the fence post where Matthew was tied, the deer that kept watch beside him, and even Matthew himself. Tears will fall as this book resonates long after the final page.

The Paladin Prophecy
Mark Frost. Random House Books for Young Readers.

Will lives a quiet, nomadic life with his parents until a test exposes his superintellectual potential. When Will's parents can no longer protect him, he escapes to a secluded private school for the extraordinarily gifted. But Will is not safe from the supernatural, ruthless forces that threaten not only him, but also the whole world.

The Pregnancy Project: A Memoir
Gaby Rodriguez with Jenna Glatzer. Simon & Schuster Books for Young Readers.

Gaby Rodriguez fakes her pregnancy and documents the reactions and stereotypes of her friends, family, and teachers who expect her to become the cliché of the low-achieving teenaged mother. The story is told with a strong voice in an attempt to stop the cycle of teen pregnancy, motherhood, and poverty.

The Raft
S.A. Bodeen. Feiwel & Friends.

Robie impulsively takes a cargo flight home to see her family on Midway Island. Tragedy ensues when the plane crashes and she finds herself in the middle of the Pacific Ocean in a leaky raft with the gravely injured copilot. Forced into survival mode, Robie examines her life and hopes for her future.

Skinny
Donna Cooner. Point.

Weighing 300 lbs. in high school is difficult. Nobody sees Ever's pretty face or hears her beautiful voice. "Skinny," the voice she hears in her head, is making things worse. Drastic action is required and a gastric bypass is planned. Can she silence the voice as the weight comes off?

Star Wars: The Ultimate Visual Guide
Ryder Windham. DK Children.

The Star Wars saga is chronicled in this revised and updated volume, which includes 40 pages of new information. Packed full of interesting facts on the ever-expanding range of books, novels, comics, and media, this is a must-read for Star Wars fans. Yes, "the force is strong within this one."

Starters
Lissa Price. Delacorte Books for Young Readers.

After surviving the Spore Wars, during which all adults ages 20–60 died, Callie is forced to provide for her ailing brother. To make money, she rents her body to the Elders who want to experience their youth again. While possessed, Callie inadvertently uncovers sinister plots that only she can stop.

Tilt
Ellen Hopkins. Margaret K. McElderry Books.

Three teens deal with the pain in their lives while finding love; however, each of their worlds tilts with deception. Mikayla struggles to find a love her parents have lost, Shane watches his parents self-destruct because of his sister's illness, and Harley desperately changes herself to gain her father's love.

Waiting
Carol Lynch Williams. Simon & Schuster.

Everything seems to fall apart when London's brother dies tragically. Without her family's support to make it through the aftermath, she seeks comfort and closure from her brother's best friend and another mysterious guy. Will things ever get better?

The Way We Fall
Megan Crewe. Hyperion Book CH.

A terrible disease ravages a small Canadian island community. Itching, fever, ticklish throat, and the loss of social inhibitions are inevitably followed by death. When the government puts the island under quarantine, people begin to lose hope. Can Kaelyn find a way to survive by forming new bonds of family and friendship.

This list has been made available to StarGroup International by the generosity of The International Reading Association. We are grateful to IRA for its dedication to ending literacy. Please visit their website at www.reading.org.

International Reading Association. (2013). Choices reading lists. Newark, DE: Author. Available at http://www.reading.org/resources/booklists.aspx. Reprinted with permission.

Resources

Alliance for Excellent Education
1201 Connecticut Ave., Suite 901
Washington, DC 20036
Tel: 202-828-0828
www.all4ed.org

The Alliance for Excellent Education is a Washington, DC-based national policy and advocacy organization that works to improve national and federal policy so that all students can achieve at high academic levels and graduate from high school ready for success in college, work, and citizenship in the twenty-first century. The Alliance focuses on America's six million most at-risk secondary school students—those in the lowest achievement quartile—who are most likely to leave school without a diploma or to graduate unprepared for a productive future. The Alliance for Excellent Education also provides economic data on the staggering costs of dropouts to society.

American Library Association
50 E Huron Street
Chicago, IL 60611
Tel: 1-800-545-2433 x 1392
www.ala.org

Founded on October 6, 1876 during the Centennial Exposition in Philadelphia, the American Library Association was created to provide leadership for the development, promotion, and improvement of library and information services and the profession of librarianship in order to enhance learning and ensure access to information for all. Our current strategic plan, ALA Ahead to 2010, calls for continued work in the areas of Advocacy and Value of the Profession, Education, Public Policy and Standards, Building the Profession, Membership and Organizational Excellence.

Books For Kids
440 Park Avenue South, 4th Floor
New York, NY 10016
Tel: 212-760-BOOK (2665)
http://www.booksforkids.org/

The mission of the Books for Kids Foundation is to promote literacy among all children with a special emphasis on low-income and at-risk preschool-aged children. Books for Kids creates libraries, donates books, and implements literacy programs to develop the critical early foundation and skills which young children need to be successful in life.

Communities In Schools
2345 Crystal Drive
 Suite 801Arlington, VA 22202
Tel: 800-CIS-4KIDS (800-247-4543)
http://www.communitiesinschools.org/

Developed by Communities In Schools Founder and Vice Chairman Bill Milliken, the "Five Basics" are a set of essentials that every child needs and deserves. Communities In Schools works to make sure that students are provided with the Five Basics, so that they have every opportunity to succeed. The Five Basics include:
1. A one-on-one relationship with a caring adult.
2. A safe place to learn and grow.
3. A healthy start and a healthy future.
4. A marketable skill to use upon graduation.
5. A chance to give back to peers and community.

Early Childhood Reading Group
Academic Improvement and Teacher Quality Programs (AITQ)
US Department of Education
400 Maryland Avenue, SW, Rm. 3E230
Washington, DC 20202-6200
Tel: 202-260-3793
http://www2.ed.gov

This program offers grants to support local family literacy projects that integrate early childhood education, adult literacy (adult basic and secondary-level education and instruction for English language learners), parenting education, and interactive parent and child literacy activities for low-income families with parents who are eligible for services under the Adult Education and Family Literacy Act and their children from birth through age 7. Teen parents and their children from birth through age 7 also are eligible. All participating families must be those most in need of program services.

First Book
1319 F St. NW, Suite 1000
Washington, DC 20004
Tel: 202-393-1222
http://www.firstbook.org/

First Book provides access to new books for children in need.

To date, First Book has distributed more than 90 million books and educational resources to programs and schools serving children from low-income families throughout the United States and Canada. First Book is transforming the lives of children in need and elevating the quality of education by making new, high-quality books available on an ongoing basis.

The Heart of America Foundation
401 F Street, NW Suite 325
Washington, DC 20001
Tel: 202-347-6278
http://www.heartofamerica.org/index.htm

The Heart of America Foundation® is a national nonprofit headquartered in Washington, D.C. We uniquely promote volunteer service and literacy. We aim to inspire acts of service and a love of reading by building community and providing children in need with the tools to read, succeed and make a difference.

Through the Books From The Heart® and READesign® programs, we revitalize school libraries and reading spaces in under-resourced communities into vital and vibrant centers of learning that become the heart of a school.

International Reading Association
800 Barksdale Rd.
PO Box 8139
Newark, DE 19714-8139
Tel: 1-800-336-7323
302-731-1600
www.reading.org

Since 1956, IRA has been a nonprofit, global network of individuals and institutions committed to worldwide literacy. More than 60,000 members strong, the Association supports literacy professionals through a wide range of resources, advocacy efforts, volunteerism, and professional development activities. Our members promote high levels of literacy for all by:
1. Improving the quality of reading instruction
2. Disseminating research and information about reading
3. Encouraging the lifetime reading habit

Jumpstart

308 Congress Street, 6th Floor
Boston, MA 02210
Tel: 617.542.5867
http://www.jstart.org/

Jumpstart's research-based, cost-effective program trains college students and community volunteers to serve preschool-age children in low-income neighborhoods. Through our proven curriculum, these children develop the language and literacy skills they need to be ready for school, setting them on the path for lifelong success. Since 1993, Jumpstart has trained 28,000 college students and community volunteers to transform the lives of 50,000 preschool children nationwide. These Corps members help children cultivate a life-long love for language and learning and ultimately provide a foundation for future success.

The Literacy Company

13901 N. 73rd St. Suite 201
Scottsdale, AZ 85260, USA
Tel: 866-732-3327
http://www.EfficientReading.com/

The Literacy Company is the developer of The Reader's Edge® software that teaches Efficient Reading skills. Efficient Readers read better & faster with improved comprehension, retention and recall. The Reader's Edge is used in 120 countries by individuals of all ages, K-16 schools, corporations and governmental organizations. Richard Sutz, The Literacy Company's founder & CEO is the author of Speed Reading (efficient reading) For Dummies.

Military Child Education Coalition
909 Mountain Lion Circle
Harker Heights, TX 76548
Tel: 254-953-1923
http://www.militarychild.org/

The Military Child Education Coalition's goal is to serve as a model of positive leadership and advocacy for ensuring inclusive, quality educational opportunities for all military-connected children. In order to ensure inclusive, quality educational experiences for all military-connected children affected by mobility, family separation, and transition, the Military Child Education Coalition will: 1) provide responsive and relevant support systems, resources, and products, 2) expand the MCEC's outreach through engagement, advocacy, and partnerships, 3) execute a strategic communications plan, and 4) build a strong, sustainable, and financially sound organization.

National Association for the Education of Young Children
1313 L Street, NW, Suite 500
Washington, DC 20005
Tel: 202-232-8777
800-424-2460 or 866-NAEYC-4U
www.naeyc.org

NAEYC has led the way toward excellence in early childhood education. Our nearly 90,000 members are teachers, administrators, parents, educators, policy makers, and others committed to bringing high-quality early education and care to all young children.

National Center for Family Literacy

325 West Main Street, Suite 300
Louisville, KY 40202
Tel: 502-584-1133
www.famlit.org

NCFL is a leading national nonprofit organization with an incredible mission: we are building a more literate and prosperous nation by helping parents and children learn together. For 20 years, NCFL has seen the power of family literacy in action. Since 1989, more than 1 million families have made education and economic progress as a result of NCFL's work.

•

National Education Association

1201 16th Street, NW
Washington, DC 20036-3290
Tel: 202-833-4000
www.nea.org

We, the members of the National Education Association of the United States, are the voice of education professionals. Our work is fundamental to the nation, and we accept the profound trust placed in us.
Our vision is a great public school for every student.
Our mission is to advocate for education professionals and to unite our members and the nation to fulfill the promise of public education to prepare every student to succeed in a diverse and interdependent world.

Education is the gateway to opportunity. All students have the human and civil right to a quality public education that develops their potential, independence, and character.
NEA also believes every student in America, regardless of family income or place of residence, deserves a quality education. In

pursuing its mission, NEA has determined that we will focus the energy and resources of our 3.2 million members on improving the quality of teaching, increasing student achievement and making schools safer, better places to learn.

The National Institute for Literacy

1775 I Street, NW; Suite 730
Washington, DC 20006-2401
Tel: 202-233-2025
www.nifl.org

Since its creation in 1991, the National Institute for Literacy has served as a catalyst for improving opportunities for adults, youth, and children to thrive in a progressively literate world. At the Institute, literacy is broadly viewed as more than just an individual's ability to read. Literacy is an individual's ability to read, write, speak in English, compute, and solve problems at levels of proficiency necessary to function on the job, in the family, and in society. The Institute, a federal agency, was established by the National Literacy Act and reauthorized in 1998 by the Workforce Investment Act.

Palm Beach County Literacy Coalition

3651 Quantum Blvd.
Boynton Beach, FL 33426
Tel: 561-279-9103
http://www.literacypbc.org/

The mission of the Literacy Coalition of Palm Beach County is to improve the quality of life in our community by promoting and achieving literacy. We serve the mother who can't read a letter sent home by her daughter's teacher, the worker who claims he left his glasses at home rather than admit he can't read the instructions left by his boss, the preschool child who lives in a home that doesn't contain a single book and the family who lives in poverty because the parents don't have the literacy skills to qualify for a job that pays a family sustaining wage. Our goal is to ensure that every child and every adult in Palm Beach County becomes a reader.

Oklahoma A+ Schools at the University of Central Oklahoma
100 North University Drive, Campus Box 97
Edmond, OK 73034
Tel: 405-974-3779
http://www.okaplus.org

Oklahoma A+ Schools is the state's research-based whole school network with a mission of nurturing creativity in every learner. OKA+ provides schools with ongoing professional development, an intricate network of support, and an active research component conducted by university professors. Spanning the state and growing every year, this network represents every kind of school from early childhood through high school, in urban, suburban and rural Oklahoma, reflecting the diversity found in communities across the state.

Pizza Hut BOOK IT! Program
P. O. Box 2999
Wichita, KS 67201
Tel: 800-426-6548
http://pizzahut.com/bookit

BOOK IT! motivates children to read by rewarding their reading accomplishments with praise, recognition and pizza. The program is simple for the teacher to use, flexible because goals match reading ability, and fun because achieving a goal is a great reason to celebrate! BOOK IT! was created in 1985 and currently reaches over 14 million students in 38,000 elementary classrooms annually.

Reach Out and Read
56 Roland Street, Suite 100D
Boston, MA 02129
Tel: 617-455-0600
http://www.reachoutandread.org

Reach Out and Read is an evidence-based nonprofit organization that promotes early literacy and school readiness in pediatric exam rooms nationwide by giving new books to children and advice to parents about the importance of reading aloud.

Reading Is Fundamental (RIF)
P.O. Box 33728
Washington, DC 20033
Tel: 202-536-3400 or 1-877-RIF-READ
http://www.rif.org/us/about-rif.htm

Reading Is Fundamental (RIF) is the largest children's literacy nonprofit in the United States. We prepare and motivate children to read by delivering free books and literacy resources to those children and families who need them most. We inspire children to be lifelong readers through the power of choice. RIF provides new, free books for children to choose from and make their own. The seeds of inspiration in these books have motivated children to follow their dreams and achieve their potential. Yes, it seems incredible for a book to launch a life, but it happens every day as hungry, inquisitive young minds reach out and grab hold of the new people, places, and ideas that books bring them.

The School Superintendents Association
1615 Duke Street
Alexandria, VA 22314
Tel: 703-528-0700
http://www.aasa.org/

AASA members are the chief education advocates for children. AASA members advance the goals of public education and champion children's causes in their districts and nationwide. As school system leaders, AASA members set the pace for academic achievement. They shape policy, oversee its implementation and represent school districts to the public at large.

Smarter Learning Group
4011 Yoke Drive
Hampstead, MD 21074
Tel: 443-986-1275
http:// www.smarterlearninggroup.com

The Smarter Learning group is dedicated to helping nonprofits, foundations, and school districts develop, grow, and sustain quality learning opportunities for young people. They provide the following specialized services: program expansion, sustainability & replication, resource development, advocacy & government relations, policy development, strategic planning, public speaking, research and evaluation, and marketing and communications.

United Through Reading
11750 Sorrento Valley Road
Suite 100
San Diego, CA 92121
Tel: 858-481-READ (7323)
http://www.unitedthroughreading.org/

Founded in 1989, United Through Reading is a nonprofit 501 (c)(3) public benefit organization. Their mission is to unite military families facing physical separation by facilitating the bonding experience of reading aloud together. United Through Reading is the nation's first nonprofit to promote the read-aloud experience for separated military families. United Through Reading offers deployed parents the opportunity to be video-recorded reading storybooks to their children which eases the stress of separation, maintains positive emotional connections and cultivates a love of reading. At nearly 200 recording locations worldwide, Marines, Soldiers and Sailors, National Guard, Reservists and Airmen, can read to their children from units on ships, in tents in Afghanistan, on bases and installations around the world and at 70 USO centers worldwide. Over one and a half million military parents, spouses and children have benefited from the program since its inception.

Other Reading Websites

http://www.babyzone.com

http://www.bblocks.samhsa.gov

http://www.begintoread.com

http://classroom.jc-schools.net

http://www.ed.gov/

http://www.educationworld.com

http://www.familyreading.org

http://www.internet4classrooms.com

http://www.modernmom.com

http://oldfashionedliving.com

http://pnla.org

http://www.readingrockets.org

http://www2.scholastic.com

http://school.familyeducation.com

http://www.teachersfirst.com

Brenda Star,

President and Chief Executive Officer,
StarGroup International

Brenda Star is president/founder of StarGroup International. She began her career with a thriving Kool-Aid and cotton candy concession stand at the age of six. From her teen years on, she established a chain of 23 ballet schools, designed and marketed a line of costume jewelry, authored a national syndicated cooking column and newsletter, established a state-wide commercial real estate company, PR and marketing firm and publishing house. She has authored numerous educational books.

An avid reader, writer, and true bibliophile, Brenda added two book divisions to her PR and marketing firm, StarGroup International. StarGroup Books specializes in educational books, and StarGroup Producer is a custom book division which specializes in producing books that are used for marketing, media and fundraising. Proud mother to two daughters and grandmother of four, she aspires to continue creating books that make a difference and inspire hope in her readers.

StarGroup International is a PR & Marketing company with two book publishing divisions. StarGroup Books specializes in publishing and marketing educational books. Star Book Producer is a custom book division, specializing in books to be used as marketing, media and fund raising tools, in addition to family and corporate histories.

For over two decades, StarGroup has maintained access to the best researchers, writers, editors, proofreaders, designers and printers in the industry, while also supplying public relations and marketing services.

Contact Us

For additional information:

StarGroup International, Inc.
1194 Old Dixie Highway, Suite 201
West Palm Beach, FL 33403

(561) 547-0667

www.stargroupinternational.com
e-mail: info@stargroupinternational.com